Stonewall + 50

TRUE STORIES OF POWER, PRIDE, AND PROGRESS

Edited by Edward McCann

Read650 | Where Writers read

Founder / Editor • Edward McCann
Executive Producer • Richard Kollath
Senior Editor • Steven Lewis
Marketing and Communications • Jane Kaupp
Design Director • Diane Fokas
Technical Advisor • Conrad Trautmann
Technical Advisor • Stephen Kaupp
Director of Photography • Kevin O'Connor
Videography/Photography • Sara Caldwell
Chief Audio Engineer • Jesse Chason
Copy Editor • Shelley Sadler Kenney

Advisory Committee
Rachel Aydt, Laura Shaine Cunningham,
Angela Davis-Gardner, Joseph Goodrich,
Jeremiah Horrigan, Arif Ilahi Khan, David Masello,
Honor Molloy, Irene O'Garden, John Pielmeier,
Susan Ragusa, James Russek, Angela Derecas Taylor,
Julie Trelstad, and Gretchen Reed

"This was the Rosa Parks moment, the time that gay people stood up and said no. And once that happened, the whole house of cards that was the system of oppression of gay people started to crumble."

— Lucian Truscott, IV, Reporter, The Village Voice

ABOUT READ650

Like many revolutions, the Stonewall uprising began spontaneously in a tiny place no one had ever heard of. It set in motion a chain of events leading to gains for the LGBTQ community—including legally recognized marriage—that seemed inconceivable fifty years ago.

The fight for these rights didn't begin with Stonewall, but Stonewall ignited a flame that grew brighter in the decades that followed, illuminating a path forward—and illuminating a people. The reverberations from those five days of outrage and resistance have echoed through American history to this day, directly and indirectly impacting the lives of the contributors to this volume.

Read650 is a literary nonprofit with a mission to promote writers through live performances that celebrate the spoken word. It's a literary forum featuring two-page, 650-word personal stories that can be performed in five minutes. Our events are organized around single, broad topics inviting a range of expression, with recorded performances added to a growing digital archive of writers reading their work aloud. The writers and their work will receive additional exposure through podcasts, broadcasts, our YouTube channel, and in printed volumes like the one you hold in your hand—a collection of pieces originally performed on stage at City Winery in downtown Manhattan.

Read650 features graduate students and grandparents, first-timers sharing a stage with bestselling authors. It's all about the writing—word choices, the shape of sentences and paragraphs, the arc of a narrative, and the poetry of a unique literary voice. To submit your work or attend our shows, visit our website or Facebook page, and join our mailing list.

Please tell your friends about us, and spread the word about the spoken word.

Ed McCann

Edward McCann, Founder / Editor

READ650.COM
FACEBOOK.COM/READ650

CONTENTS

Stonewall + 50

TRUE STORIES OF POWER, PRIDE, AND PROGRESS

Edited by Edward McCann

JANE MARX

Jane Marx began her career in teaching as a tenth-grade social studies teacher; she then switched to publishing and worked as
a social science editor at Random House. Next, she became a student
at the American Academy of Dramatic Arts. She's been a self-em-
ployed New York City tourist guide for nearly forty years, and is also
a stand-up comic, storyteller, actor, and writer. She's written and
performed in two solo plays, *A Coffin Turning Clockwise: A Comedy in
Real Time* in 2017 and *Til My Last Breath* in 2018, both produced by
Artistic New Directions Theatre Company. Conscious she's a human
dynamo dependent upon energy for her existence, Jane wishes to die
from exhausting her potential.

ORIGINAL THINKERS

Jane Marx

Say it aloud, "That's how I feel." Immediately you're declaring yourself a sentient being, entitled to your emotions no matter what they be.

But if you're gay, and it's the 1960s, you've got your work cut out. There's homophobic legislation everywhere, forcing you in the closet one minute, leading you to decide to step out the next. Having a drink at a bar with others of your ilk. Watching the police raid the place. Shaking off your cowering position. You rise up, fists clenched at last. You defend yourself inside the Stonewall Inn: June 28, 1969.

Yet, I'm tone-deaf then, obsessed with getting troops out of Vietnam. My brother's bailiwick is gay liberation. He's in Cambridge, Massachusetts, getting his master's in city planning at the Harvard School of Design, gifted with a $5,000 Housing and Urban Development fellowship.

My father's proud, patting him on the shoulder, giving him a hug. It's a far cry from those chastising days when my father berated him for not liking baseball, dragging him off Saturday mornings to be a catcher in a Little League team; distaste was written all over my brother's face. My father, irate when my brother drops the ball,

1

resolves he'll make a man of him yet. After all, his boy's the son of a left fielder.

But our father's plan gets aborted. My brother writes a note. "I hate baseball. I don't want to play it ever again." He leaves it in my mother's night table drawer, and that's that. He's doing what he likes, collecting stamps; drawing maps of imaginary cities; writing aerogrammes to Finnish and French pen pals.

I'm twenty-four and he's twenty-one in 1968, the year before Stonewall, when he tells me he's gay—on the down-low, confidentially. He says, "Don't tell Mother or Dad; they'll both be ashamed. Dad will blame Mother for making me soft; Mother will get scared."

I'm listening, seeing this as all bad. I've already classified myself as weird, waiting for a sign when I know myself. According to my Dad, I'm perpetually chasing my tail. It's impossible for me to think before I speak; I've got nothing to ruminate upon. Experiencing two eye operations at five and getting molested at seven, I'm half shut-down.

But I'm grateful my brother's my friend. He appears so mainstream—until this. I ask, "Does your girlfriend Christine know?" He says, "She has to. I tell her I dream of penises, not her."

Which is why he may have been inside the Stonewall Inn at some time in his life. He's in Manhattan a lot, staying at my place. I know his drill: The Mine Shaft. Rawhide. St. Mark's Baths. Once, after perusing the Ramble, he informs me, nonchalantly, that a mugger there took his watch—the one I give him for his college graduation. I'm furious. I say, "Next time whack off in the shower. The worst that can happen, you'll slip."

With him, I'm myself. I even ask, "Do you think I'm crazy?" "No," he assures me. "You're an original thinker. Trust yourself. Carry an imaginary machete. Cut down what's in your way. Be on your own path."

2

And just like that. I'm on track. We two, in our Hansel and Gretel bond, each parenting the other. Reducing each other's stress. All of this coming to an end with a single diagnosis in May 1987. I'm with him inside his doctor's office. I see black.

He loses weight, apprising our parents, "Chagas, schistoso-miasis, myocarditis, the diseases I got in the Peace Corps in Brazil. They're back."

He dies March 11, 1989, his body atop his bed inside the Harvard Infirmary. Blind. One hundred pounds on a six-foot frame. Friends, students say goodbye. His last words etched inside my head. "For the last fifteen years, I've not been depressed. Not once."

DAVID MASELLO

David Masello moved to New York from Evanston, Illinois, and has made his living as a writer and editor for more than thirty years. He began his career as a nonfiction book editor at Simon & Schuster, then went on to hold senior editorial positions at many magazines, including *Travel + Leisure, Art & Antiques,* and *Town & Country,* where he was features editor. He's currently executive editor of *Milieu,* a magazine about design and architecture. He's a widely published essayist and poet, with pieces appearing in the *New York Times,* Salon, *Best American Essays,* and numerous literary and art magazines. His plays have been produced and performed by the Manhattan Repertory Theatre, Jewish Women's Theatre of Los Angeles, Big Apple Theater Festival, and Fresh Fruit Festival. He is the author of two books about art and architecture.

4

PASS-THROUGH BY DAVID MASELLO

David Masello

From the kitchen counter, I see my friend framed by the pass-through that links me to the living/dining room. Twenty-plus years in this apartment, I've had an inside view of my life through this rectangular cut-out.

A Labor Day weekend, I've assembled the ingredients I need to fulfill a wish—Sunday, September, hint of dusk, Respighi's Botticelli Suite, salt of sweat from our walk together over the Brooklyn Bridge. Friends, we're so comfortable with that identity that he reads on the sofa beneath a funnel of lamplight while I unwrap and stir, mix and marinate.

Just days earlier, on the deck of the upstate rental I'd had for the summer—that last afternoon before packing up and retracing the Taconic, its narrow shoulders dotting with deer I fear will leap—I intoned my annual wish: that the coming season would include this very scene, with him, or, since I must, with someone. And there he is, framed within the recess like a painting, but no composition made of living parts holds.

As suddenly as I'd spotted flashes of reddened leaves atop

trees the drive back, signaling seasonal change, I've had a change of feelings for him, which I cannot admit. If stated, the words would undo this, and he would vanish from my frame.

Of the seven Manhattan apartments I've occupied, this one has the best view, not just outside the windows, but within. Through my pass-through, I've witnessed many scenes I've composed, an ever-changing art gallery.

Handing my former mother-in-law, in celebration of her art show, a third martini with pimento-stuffed olives rolling at the bottom like tropical fish. The turkeys I've carved, lasagnas I've segmented, rosés I've uncorked, as I pass drinks and plates through to those gathered in the room beyond. I see my now-late uncle at Easter, frail, excusing himself to lie down, and my then boyfriend bringing him water I handed through that pass-through. The interior-fireworks one Fourth of July when a drunken acquaintance grabbed the youngest guest and kissed him so hard he drew blood, the guest dabbing his lip in astonishment, my handing him a damp cloth through the opening, he handing it back for rinsing. Halloween when a handsome self-proclaimed witch came to dinner, his pentagram wrist-tattoo revealed as he smoothed the tablecloth; was my date Rosemary's Baby all grown-up?

I host an annual Christmas Eve dinner, the "Stray Gays", many of us professing to seek people exactly like each other, but few acting on each other. I'm telling you, that's the mystery of gay middle-aged men; what we want, and who, is exactly before us without taking it. Maybe it's because we recognize friends as family, especially at our age—and why risk losing a friend for something as hazardous as romance. I've yet to meet a gay man who's fallen for someone who was his friend first. I'm pioneer stock.

As for the framed scene of him, never before have my feelings for a friend shifted this way. And falling in love with a friend: taboo as incest.

"Look," I call to him, at the pass-through, wanting him to see what's happening. The swath of Midtown outside my windows is ablaze with the changing September light, its sharpness bringing into relief a barge sliding by on the river, a dog barking from its deck, *Halifax* stenciled in monumental font along the hull.

He, however, doesn't remain in that light. You know you love someone when you start to love what they do. With him: monumental sculpture. An aluminum beam we saw together in a sculpture-park meadow, suddenly for me, beautiful as a Bernini. Upon discerning, later, what I feel, he dismisses me, us. He prefers artworks abstract; I, realistic.

But as that meal progresses, he lowers the novel to look at me and I gaze at him, opposite sides of the pass-through—though at the table, soon, we will convene, not so unlike a couple.

ANN LEVIN

Ann Levin is a writer and editor. She was the national news editor at The Associated Press, where she worked for twenty years. Before that she reported for a number of newspapers, among them being the *San Diego Tribune*. She has also written for *USA Today*, *AARP*, *The Forward* and other publications. Ann served as an editor for the UN Population Fund and Columbia University. She lives in New York City with her photographer husband, Stan Honda, and is currently working on a memoir.

LESBIAN NATION

Ann Levin

Jill Johnston was the first woman I ever had a crush on.

She wrote for the *Village Voice*, and I read her columns religiously. They were lyrical and profane, written in stream-of-consciousness style. She used minimal punctuation, spelled amerika lowercase and with a *k*, and had a knack for saying outrageous things.

Like, "All women are lesbians except those who don't know it." And, "Until all women are lesbians, there will be no true political revolution." And, "Lesbian is a label invented ... to throw at any woman who dares to be a man's equal."

In 1973 Jill came to Smith College to talk about her new book, *Lesbian Nation*. She was forty-four, and I was nineteen, a sophomore majoring in English.

The year before, I'd read Kate Millett's *Sexual Politics*, which shattered everything I thought I knew about English literature. It turned me into a militant feminist and made me understand that Norman Mailer—then the darling of the literary establishment—was a creep and possibly a psychopath. I didn't know who I was or what

9

I wanted out of life, but I knew that I had no interest in Amherst College mixers, where girls drank until they blacked out and woke up in strange beds next to a pile of coats.

Jill arrived on our well-behaved campus like an Amazon warrior, surrounded by her all-female entourage. Tall and rangy, with shaggy hair to her shoulders and small, crooked teeth, she had the confidence of a jock—like Billie Jean and Martina—and the goofy charm of a clown. Just by looking at her, you could tell how comfortable she felt in her body, and if you didn't like the way she looked, well, too bad.

At the end of her talk, I stuck around for an autograph, and when it was time for her to go, she gave me a jaunty wave and said, in a slightly snarky voice, "See you around the campus."

I swooned.

Fast forward forty-four years, and despite my crush on Jill, I've been married for thirty years to a man.

I'm downtown, at a play about a notorious debate in 1971 at Town Hall in New York City. The topic: women's liberation. The moderator: Norman Mailer. On the panel: Jill Johnston.

As the actors recite their parts, film footage of the event plays on a screen. And there's Jill, reciting her poetry at the podium. Two women barge on stage, and all three tumble to the floor and start to make out.

After the play, I rushed home to see if I could find my copy of Lesbian Nation. It was long gone, left behind in a move. I emailed a woman down the hall, a well-known feminist back in the day. She said her copy was missing, too. When I went online to buy it, I discovered it was out of print. Even the Strand didn't have it.

Next, I emailed the New York Public Library, but they kept their copy off-site. Finally, I realized there was only one place to find it – the Lesbian Herstory Archives in Brooklyn. And so, on a blustery day in early spring, I took the F train out to Park Slope.

And, sure enough, there it was, sitting on a shelf in a yellowing cover, with a picture of Jill in an embroidered denim jacket and a metal necklace the size of a bicycle gear.

As I sat down and flipped through the pages, I realized that pretty much everything she'd said about the patriarchy was still true. At the women's march in 2017, aging feminists like me, with gray hair and no makeup, carried signs that said, "I can't believe we still have to protest this shit."

Long ago, Jill argued that who you sleep with is a political decision. I had no problem with that. I just failed at being a lesbian.

JOSE L. PENA

Jose L. Pena was born in Montevideo, Uruguay. He graduated from the schools of Medicine and Science in Uruguay with a PhD in neuroscience. He later obtained a Pew Latin America postdoctoral fellowship to conduct research at the California Institute of Technology from 1994 to 1997. Eventually, he became a senior research fellow at Caltech, in Pasadena, California. In 2005, he became a faculty member in the Department of Neuroscience at Albert Einstein College of Medicine in New York, where he was recently named a tenured professor of neuroscience. He lives in New York City and has a small house in the Massachusetts Berkshires where he has positioned perches on nearby trees for owls, one of his favorite subjects of study.

A BIRD'S-EYE VIEW

Jose L. Pena

Mom walked in my bedroom and sat on my bed in our home in Montevideo. She started caressing my hair. "Jose, you sometimes behave as something you are not." I was around the age of ten—yet knew what she meant. I had already been called sissy (maricon) in school and sensed dislike on people's faces when I let my spontaneous self show.

Years later she cried when I told her the reason I was out the previous night was because I'd stayed at the hospital with a friend dying of AIDS. She was crying about me, not about my friend, upset by the implicit indication that I was gay. Sadly, her early Alzheimer's did not allow us to revisit these memories as adults.

When I was in my twenties, Dad called me into his office the day after all the gay bars in Montevideo were raided. Every man in every one of those places had been arrested and taken to the police station for questioning on a criminal case involving a relative of the country's president.

"Jose, how did you end up in jail last night?" my father asked. "Be careful who you go out with. I know good psychiatrists whom I

13

can put you in touch with if needed."

He was proud, however, the day I came down with gonorrhea. Oh, the satisfaction in his face while injecting me with penicillin and joking about my presumed adventures with female prostitutes; This episode became a bonding experience in our father-son relationship.

Not only do my Dad and I look still alike and carry the same first, middle, and last names, but I also decided to become a doctor, too. But midway into medical school training, I realized I'd be a better scientist than a doctor. It was easier for me to face reality when dealing with a guinea pig than a person. In my workplaces, however, I kept blushing when colleagues lamented, "I haven't had a puto minute to run a puto experiment." Puto, faggot, is not an uncommon expression in my native country of Uruguay. That blushing went away when a few years later I arrived in California as a postdoctoral fellow and saw guys holding hands on the street. I went back home then but nothing was the same after having experienced comfort with my identity and the marvels of the United States' academic environments. And here I am now, studying the brains of barn owls. People ask me, "Why that choice?" The simplest answer is that I'm fascinated by brains that are not close to ours, yet reveal universal laws of nature, just as astrophysicists are absorbed by planets and stars in other galaxies.

Being a gay neuroscientist is often a rather lonely endeavor; it's hard to find role models among colleagues. I often wish my male colleagues stopped pushing me to conform to masculine standards of leadership and success, and confusing my kindness with being bendable. Still, growing up as a gay boy taught me how to read people's faces and switch from Venus to Mars in a wink, which has helped.

Things have turned out all right for a self-professed gay Latino nerd who's managed to act on principle. Investigating owls inspires me daily and has given me a bird's-eye view of human dealings, especially in these times when we can't stop hearing about building walls to keep out people from countries like mine, though I think of myself as an open door.

Was growing up gay in my Latin American country of Uruguay different than growing up here? I just know what I experienced where I lived. But now that I'm an adult and live here, I have some perspective. Just the other day my sister texted, asking if the "puto" book she had ordered arrived. I smiled, and replied "By puto you mean wonderful, right?—I'll check the order status of that book."

LINDA SHAPIRO

Linda Shapiro attended Boston University, The New School, and received a BA from the College of New Rochelle. She studied modern dance at the Martha Graham School in New York City and taught modern dance while raising her daughters. Linda eventually had a business career in the outdoor industry and travelled abroad as an importer, writing—always writing—wherever she travelled. Linda takes writing classes at the Writing Institute at Sarah Lawrence College and writes with The Scarsdale Library Writing group. Her short story, "*At the* Beach," was recently published by ForthMagazine.Com.

CHICKEN SOUP FOR HOWIE

Linda Shapiro

The call from my brother, Howie, came early in the morning. He's been travelling and is home in San Francisco.

"Hi Lin."

"How was your trip? I ask.

"Okay, just left me tired, a sore throat, but I'm coming to New York next week."

"Great," I say, hoping he doesn't have strep. "I'm sure you'll be better by then."

The day before he arrives I buy parsnips, carrots, celery, onions, dill, and parsley, ingredients for Grandma Fanny's chicken soup. I chop the celery and carrots and add them to the pot. As the steam rises, I think about Howie the teenager. He lived with me after our mother died.

"Take care of Howie," my mother had said. Suddenly, I became more than a big sister.

The sweet smell of soup fills the kitchen. I add kosher chicken, extra broth, and taste, like my grandmother did. I add salt and dill. The next day, when I leave for the airport, I take a water bottle for

Howie, and cut up an apple.

I look for Howie at the arrival gate. Howie, six feet, two inches, light brown hair appears. I see his handsome face instantly, his back-pack hanging off his shoulder. He bends down to hug me. It's been that way since he was thirteen, taller than I am, having to bend down to meet my petite frame. As soon as we're in the car, I glance at him for a second.

"How are you feeling?"

"Not sure, about the same."

"I've got chicken soup for you."

He shrugs his shoulders the way he did when he was a boy and didn't want to answer. He used to follow me around with my friends, staying close by my side.

Howie is quiet on the ride home from the airport. He sips wa-ter, takes a few bites of the apple and then puts his head back to rest. When we arrive at my house he's almost asleep.

"We're here," I say

In the house, Howie drops his bag on the floor and flops down on the couch in the living room. I head for the kitchen to heat the soup. When it's ready I bring him a bowl. He sits up and looks at me.

"Listen Lin, my friend Ari's not well. It started as a sore throat."

"I'm sorry. I remember Ari, wearing his white silk yoga robe."

Howie smiled for a second. "I'm worried, the doctor's worried. Tom and Bob are ill, too"

If he said the word AIDS that day I didn't hear it or know what it meant. Now that I think back, he must have. It was 1982.

For the moment now, it's 1962. Howie is sixteen. I'm doing laundry. I pick up his ripped jeans and a Comfort Inn Motel receipt falls out of the pocket. I realize that he must have slept there with his camp friend, William, instead of staying at Eddie's house, like he had told me. I'm angry, confused, and afraid. I don't let him know what I suspect. Instead I go to the family doctor. "It's okay," Dr. Philips says.

I didn't hug Howie or tell him it's okay after finding the receipt or talking to Dr. Philips. That's when people whispered, kept secrets. I stayed silent.

But now, here we are in my living room and Howie's not feeling well. He came anyway. This isn't like when he left a motel receipt in his pocket. He's here, next to me. "We'll call doctors in New York. Maybe you just need rest. We'll get you better." I don't yet understand the agony that lies ahead. I sit next to him on the couch, hold his hand. I smell the soup. I wonder if it's boiling. "I'll be right back Howie. I'm coming right back." I run into the kitchen to turn off the stove.

JOHN PIELMEIER

John Pielmeier began his career with the play and movie *Agnes of God*. Since then he's had three more plays mounted on Broadway and over twenty-five film, television movies and miniseries produced. His stage adaptation of *The Exorcist* will be coming to New York next season. Scribner published his first novel, *Hook's Tale*, to wonderful reviews, and he's recently adapted it as a two-person play, premiering in Houston in 2020. He's received the Humanitas Award (plus two nominations), five Writers' Guild Award nominations, a Gemini nomination, an Edgar Award, Camie Award, and a Christopher Award. His projects have also won a Gemini Award and have been nominated for the Emmy Award and the Golden Globe Award.

GIRLFRIENDS

John Pielmeier

Their names were Mart and Alison and they came to visit us
on occasion when I was a boy, and once or twice we went to visit
them. They were school teachers and lived together on the top floor
of an old brick house. Mart was tall and thin and wore her dark hair
in a bun; Alison was shorter and red-haired and was the kind of
woman once called "handsome." Her full name was Alison Doug-
las, which translated in my five-year-old mind as "Alice and Doug-
las", but my mother referred to them as "Mart and Alison" —which
sounded to me like Martin Alison. It was all so confusing, but oddly
appropriate, their names linked as though they were one person, half
female, half male, which strikes me even today as not incorrect.

Most of my mother's girlfriends were of the same physical
mold. They were either thin and wiry or square and muscular, and
all of them were unmarried but for one who had several children
and a mustache. Most were gym teachers and my mother would
describe them as "outdoorsy." They first met when she worked as a
secretary for the Girl Scouts; they were leaders and administrators,
and they were all very fond of her. Whenever they visited, she wel-

comed them with a kindness shadowed by a certain reluctance I never completely understood. I liked them; they were fun to be around, and they were comfortable in their bodies in ways that other women weren't. They were independent, and they seemed happy.

My mother and her girlfriends spent the summers of the 1930's at a Girl Scout camp near their hometown. All were camp counsellors, and they bonded, I imagine, sitting around a campfire late at night after their young charges were in bed, talking of the girls and their teenage problems, and celebrating their own love of being in the great outdoors away from civilization and the tyranny of men.

My mother's boss, a woman named Billie, introduced my mother to my father, and my mother always spoke of Billie with great affection, still remembering the sorrow she suffered when Billie moved to another city and another Girl Scout office. She and Billie exchanged Christmas cards every year, and when I was grown I arranged for my mother and Billie to reconnect. I met Billie for the first time then: she was square and muscular and very outdoorsy. My mother was happy to see her, but the meeting was a little awkward: they didn't have a lot to say to each other and they never saw one another again.

Our next-door neighbor Georgetta once referred to one of my mother's girlfriends as a lesbian. Mother was incensed. It was as if Georgetta had accused the woman, in the paranoia of the 1950's, of being a Russian spy. Of course, in the spirit of that metaphor, all of my mother's girlfriends spoke with thick Russian accents; still, my mother refused to recognize their foreign allegiance. Her Catholicism, and the tenor of the times, denied these women approval. But when her closest friend—a solid woman named Marian who had a contagious laugh and eyes that squinted with warmth—when Marian moved in with another woman, my mother refused to judge her. She prayed for her, I'm certain, but she always welcomed Marian gladly when her friend came to visit.

The happiest six months of my mother's life was when she served as a substitute girls' gym teacher at my high school. The girls confided in her, and they loved her. Years later, when my wife and I celebrated our tenth anniversary with a party and a dance, my mother spent the evening cutting a rug with a female friend of ours. "Your mother's a terrific dancer," our friend told us later. "She would have made a great lesbian."

KATHRYN MAYER

Kathryn Mayer—Kate—is a potty-mouth writer, humorist, and activist writing out loud with humor and angst about social issues, parenting, midlife, and sadly, gun violence prevention at www. kathrinmayer.com. She is occasionally funny on Instagram & Twitter @kathykatemayer, and plays well with others on Facebook. She's a reluctant inductee into AARP, mom of four almost grown-and-flown kids, and an aspiring writer with rejections to prove it. Her blog, *Writing out Loud*, is a National Society of Newspaper Columnist award winner, and received CT Press Club Best Personal Blog in Connecticut, and BlogHer Voice of the Year honors. Her essays appear on-line, in-print, and most often, on fridges sticky with smiles and swears.

TWO GUYS IN THE BACK OF A TRUCK
Kathryn Mayer

In the seventies, I spent weekends wandering up and down dirty aisles of flea markets, antique shows, and auction halls that smelled like funnel cake, barn animals, and old lady purses.

Instead of soccer, softball or dance, my childhood was spent picking through attics, boxes, basements, and trunks of cars for photography, tin toys, local memorabilia, rag dolls. Quirky collectibles. Unique, clever, saleable: buy low, sell high.

Mom and Dad supplemented their teacher salaries buying and selling antiques, so I was inducted at an early age into the weird, wonderful world of wickedly smart people, nomads, and long before the alphabet soup even existed, the LGBTQ community.

I had a good eye. My mom would give me a fist full of twenties, her tax ID number, and send me on my way picking the fields of Stormville, Brimfield, or street fairs in New York.

Dealers eyeballed the dirty little kid dressed like she just rolled out of the back of a van, because often that's exactly what I did: antique dealers often sleep in their cars to get an early start on selling, and more importantly, buying.

"Can I help you, little girl?"

"Just looking," I said, often mistaken for a pain-in-the-ass kid, the you-break-it-you-bought-it type, or worse, a shoplifter.

But all that changed when I unrolled a fist of cash and asked, "What's the dealer price on this? How much for cash?"

Once I was picking Brimfield with my mom late in the day—customers gone, dealers now relaxing, cooking on little hibachi's, drinking bottles of sweaty beer. While thumbing through a box of tintypes, looking for anything absurd: dead people, civil war soldiers, circus freaks, animals—I looked up to find two men, GROWN-UPS, legs swinging off the back of their flatbed truck. They were laughing, legs tangled, leaning into each other. One had a guitar, the other a beer. Eww, they appeared to be flirting. And then they kissed.

"Mom! Look!! What are they doing?" I gawked, elbowing her hard.

"What—them? Oooh, kissing," she said, barely glancing up, then back at a nineteenth century stoneware crock with two folksy birds intricately painted in a deep, vibrant blue.

BOYS KISSING. Didn't see that on *Little House on the Prairie*. Or *Happy Days*. Not even *The Odd Couple*!

"Stop staring, Kathy. It's none of your business."

"But, but ..."

"Listen to me, what's the problem? Here's the deal: sometimes men love women, sometimes women love men. And sometimes men love men and women love women. Maybe both. Who cares? Does it really matter? How is it any of your business?"

"Really? I just ... I didn't know. Okay, cool."

My mom made it no-big-deal, and therefore, it remained no big deal. She turned and walked away, onto the next booth, the next unexpected discovery. I stayed, seeing something my mom didn't.

"Excuse me, sir? Sir? How much?" I asked, and the dude swung off the back of the truck, came over and looked at the large photo I held out. It was a lithograph of an Indian elephant, some sort of prince or princess—I couldn't tell which—standing awkwardly next to it, staring straight into the camera, not daring to blink, uncomfortable at the spotlight shining on him or her. The costumed elephant was ever the regal, docile, and confident subject.

"This? It's a lot, you know, don't touch it. Very expensive: $150; go find your mom," he said, taking it from me and putting it out of reach.

His condescending smile dismissed a little girl out of place in a field full of dusty memories, mostly unappreciated, some undiscovered yet valuable to someone, somewhere. He turned his back and walked away.

"Is that your best?" I asked. "Any wiggle room? How 'bout a hundred dollars, cash? Right here, we got a deal?" I started peeling off twenties.

He turned back, walked over, smiled, and we got down to business.

RICHARD SELLANO

Richard Sellano is a writer, painter, and web designer. After a deep dive into healthcare as a clinical pharmacist, he pursued an MBA that gave him an entrée to the investing arena. At the financial giant, Vanguard, Rick's assignments spanned the writing of pen letters for the founding chairman to later, writing materials to promote savings for retirement. Today, Rick runs "My Ink Shines," a marketing agency he launched, and he has earned a Certification in Marketing Strategy from Cornell University. Rick is a contributor to the blog for the University of Pennsylvania's Morris Arboretum. He recently published a short story about a soldier facing a mysterious force as the man returns from Pakistan. Currently, Rick is working on a novel, *The Woman in B208*.

A SUMMER STAGE

Richard Sellano

I was a short, slight, eleven-year-old boy in the summer of 1969, a time when I happened upon a new form of self-identity. "I'm a faggot," I said to myself in our backyard. Without an idea of its meaning, I spoke and enunciated the word with conviction. I continued the proclamation as I tried to twirl around my mother's clothesline pole. I relished that backyard spot because copper-colored butterflies flitted about our nearby lilac bush. Other than reading under our big maple, which I did to nearly a compulsive excess, waltzing with the butterflies and smelling the lilacs were some of my favorite ways to spend that summer.

The announcement of my new moniker was not born from an epiphany about my sexuality. I lacked any idea about that facet of life! Understanding sex, at that point, would have required knowledgeable siblings or parents eager to launch into the topic. I'd repeat to myself, "I'm a faggot" because other boys in our neighborhood—older cocky, athletic chaps transitioning to young men with muscles—had attached that identifier to me. When this name-calling started, I didn't mind. I knew that I was different from these boys—

in obvious ways and in ones yet undiscovered.

Certain comforting truths existed on my stage of naïveté. I figured that "faggot" was a description that fit some boys, the world was all-loving and—much like the reliability of the butterflies outside—movie music was always playing in my bedroom. I was obsessed with a recording featuring my favorite performer—the soundtrack to the Julie Andrews film, *Star*. Owing to the movie's abysmal box office results, the album was nearly impossible to find. I unearthed mine in a clearance bin at Woolworth's and handily paid the twenty-five-cent cost.

A fan to the core, I adored everything Julie sang. Gertrude Lawrence and her friendship with Noel Coward—the story around which the film was wrapped—were unknowns to me. Before dinner, I lip-synched to the tunes and watched my performance in my dresser mirror. Mom, in the kitchen, had no idea that in my mind's eye I had become Ella Shields—an entertainer of early 1900s British music halls—portrayed singing, "Burlington Bertie from Bow." The jacket back's photo showed Andrews twirling an umbrella for this number. I substituted a bamboo cane I had won at the previous summer's fair.

Alone in my room, I imagined that most other boys were not having this much fun—or at least this kind of fun. And while it seemed that no one wanted to be my friend at that point, I didn't mind too much. I imagined that Julie Andrews might have been a compatriot—convinced each time her jubilant rendition of the soundtrack's "Has Anyone Seen Our Ship?" filled my spirits with helium.

The wrap-up of each summer vacation, however, delivered anxiety about the end of the hiatus and unknowns of the new school year. That year was worse. My mostly pleasant father was angry with me, his rage born from what I told my mother about me being a faggot. "It's what you call a small, weaker boy," I explained to her. My brawny father, an athlete since college, saw things differently. He said to me while spitting from both anger and the word he emphasized, that I was "sissified." He delivered it like one might state, "That hotel room is infested with bed bugs!" The emphasis was on the disgusting part. At that point, all I had was his immediate, visceral reaction—without the benefit of time and its potential to buff sharp edges. I figured that some people thought that faggots were terrible, even repulsive—but I hadn't begun to understand why. My father didn't or couldn't explain his meaning, leaving me to cling to my last summer of ignorant bliss—and that remaining week with Julie Andrews, books, flowers, and butterflies.

LISA E. DAVIS

With a PhD in comparative literature, **Lisa E. Davis** taught at SUNY Stony Brook, at York College/CUNY, and collaborated with the Center for Puerto Rican Studies at Hunter College. Her novel, *Under the Mink* (2001, 2015) recreates the 1940s world of Mafia-owned Village nightclubs. For more information, visit www.underthemink. com Her recent nonfiction chronicle of the 1949 Smith Act trial, that sent the National Board of the American Communist Party to federal prison, traces the career of the lesbian FBI informant and prosecution witness Angela Calomiris. *Undercover Girl: The Lesbian Informant Who Helped the FBI Bring Down the Communist Party* was published by Imagine Press in 2017. Both books are available on Amazon. Other highlights of her career include meeting Fidel Castro and almost drowning in the Colorado River.

TURNING THE PAGES

Lisa E. Davis

Buddy Kent seemed at home in her tailored slacks and long-sleeve shirt open at the neck, in Paris or Greenwich Village. She held a photo album on her lap and pointed.

"That was Miki Leff—she went to Paris to learn the language, then passed herself off as an Egyptian countess," she said. Buddy turned another page, to a dyke in profile and tux. "And that was Frede. Her club was Chez Frede." The accent was Brooklyn French. "Marlene Dietrich set it up for her."

Our team of LGBTQ historians, assigned to interview Buddy, an active member of SAGE (Senior Activists in a Gay Environment), about Stonewall, sighed in unison. Buddy flipped a page in her album to a dashing figure in white tie and tux.

"Who's that?" I asked.

She laughed. "That's me!...when I was a chorus boy at the 181 Club, 181 Second Avenue."

My colleagues looked bewildered. We had talked about interviewing Buddy to record the fears and frustrations of "older lesbians" before gay liberation. But she hadn't shown much interest in our questionnaire: When did you come out? What was your first sexual experience? How did the gay liberation movement change your life? Were you at Stonewall?

I asked her again what she knew about Stonewall. "I was on my way home from St. Vincent's," she began. "I'd been working as an x-ray technician at the hospital for about five years, after The Page Three closed down."

That was the club Buddy owned with Jacquie Howe, her girl-friend, and Kicky Hall, who had his own touring drag show.

"I saw the crowd," she continued, "and walked over to Sheri-dan Square. It was my neighborhood." I asked her what she thought. "It was amazing to see the gay boys give the cops a dose of their own medicine. They'd been beatin' up gay people, girls too, throwin' 'em in jail in the Village forever."

She explained that gay clubs had mob protection. They paid off the cops. But it wasn't always enough. She went on to say how there had been a big raid at the 181 because the neighbors com-plained about the boys and dykes going in and out in drag. "We had to watch our *p*'s and *q*'s—pimps and queers—after that." Buddy sud-denly looked pensive. "Somebody musta slipped up at Stonewall. Missed a payoff. Or the heat was on from the top. Maybe it was an election year. Always tryin' to clean up New York. But you know," she added in a serious tone, "we would never have come out in the streets that way if it hadn't been for the Vietnam war protests and Dr. King's Civil Rights marches in the sixties."

"Like a revolution?" I suggested.

"Long overdue, and we were proud to be part of it." With an air of nostalgia, Buddy turned back to her photo album and flipped another page.

"Who's *that*?" It was a woman walking a snake on a leash, down a city street.

Buddy laughed. "Oh, that's Zorita, the biggest strip act in New York. She worked with snakes."

"Snakes? Did this qualify as 'lesbian courage' before the gay liberation movement"?

"Yeah, Zorita made a lot of money. But snakes were not my style." She turned another page to what looked like a publicity photo of a young Buddy, one panel in tie, top hat and tails, the other stripped down to only the bare essentials. The caption read "Bubbles Kent, Exotic Dancer." A nightclub on Sullivan Street, Jimmy Kelly's.

I tried not to sound puritanical. "You had a strip act? Male to female."

"Yeah," Buddy smiled, "I guess now they'd call it trans. It was always around. The Wall Street gang, the mobsters, the Bridge-and-Tunnel crowd, that's what they came down to the Village to see. We were way ahead of our time."

Yes, there was a Village nightlife before—and way before—Stonewall.

PATRICK RYAN

Patrick Ryan is the author of the short story collection *The Dream Life of Astronauts* (named one the Best Books of the Year by the *St. Louis Times-Dispatch*, LitHub, Refinery 29, and Electric Literature) and *Send Me* (a finalist for The Center for Fiction's First Novel Prize). He is also the author of three novels for young adults. His fiction has been anthologized in *The Best American Short Stories* and has appeared in *Tin House, Crazyhorse, The Yale Review,* and elsewhere. His nonfiction has been published in Tales of Two Cities *from Middlebury Magazine, Granta,* and other anthologies. A recipient of a National Endowment for the Arts Fellowship in Fiction and the former associate editor of *Granta,* he is the current editor of *One Story.*

DEMOCRACY WAS

Patrick Ryan

1.   Democracy was being told by my mother that I shouldn't marry anyone without first living with that person for a year. Compatibility, she said, was crucial to a good marriage. I wanted to ask her if she wished she'd lived with my father for a year before marrying him, but I didn't. It was 1976, and I was eleven years old. She assumed, as I did, that I would marry a woman one day.

2.   Democracy was watching "Barney Miller" with my family and laughing at the gay characters and at the way the straight cops reacted to them. My father laughed too, but he wasn't amused when I started mincing around the living room the way the gay characters had. "You know," he said, "they didn't used to have characters like that on TV." "What about Mr. Mooney?" I asked, still mincing. "What about Uncle Arthur? What about Dr. Smith?"

3.   Democracy was discovering, upon turning eighteen, that when I did my compulsory registration for the selective service, I could also register as a conscientious objector. I told my parents my intention, and my father became irate. Only communists and homosexuals were conscientious objectors, he said. My mother defended

me, said the choice was mine.

4. Democracy was cowering with my college boyfriend in his dorm room while some other young men who lived on his floor tried to kick the door in, yelling that they would kill us both if they got in. They didn't know us but had caught on. My boyfriend called the campus police and explained the situation. The banging and shouting were so loud that he couldn't hear the response on the other end of the line. "What?" "You're just going to have to deal with this yourselves," the voice said.

5. Democracy was coming out to my recently-divorced mother when I was twenty-three and having her cry and say she was worried I'd get AIDS. And coming out to my father when I was twenty-five and having him reply, without the slightest change in his expression, "I know that. I've known since you were eighteen." I asked him how, and he said, "You're not a communist."

6. Democracy was telling my father, eleven years later, that I'd been seeing someone, that I was in love, and that it was serious. "I'm not saying I understand it," he said, "but I want you to be happy." I thanked him for that. He said, "You're welcome.

7. Democracy was arguing with my father about "Don't Ask, Don't Tell." While I clearly had no intention of ever joining the military, I said, "You think that if I were in the Army, I should have to hide who I am from my commander?" The word commander felt ridiculous on my tongue. But it didn't matter; we were having two different conversations. "What I'm saying," he told me, "is I don't think it's healthy to have homosexuals and heterosexuals in combat together." I pointed out that he'd never been in combat.

8. Democracy was one of our last conversations. He told me he thought the Defense of Marriage Act was reasonable. "How can you think that?" I asked. "I'm your son." "It should be left up to the states," he said. Appalled, I spun a scenario wherein Fred and

I were on a road trip, and as we drove across state lines, we were legally married in one state and not married in the next. Married, not married, state after state. And let's say we got into an accident in one of the anti-gay marriage states and I went to the hospital, and Fred wasn't allowed to visit me because he wasn't considered family. Was that okay? "Don't bully me," my father said. "You don't have to drive through those states. Who's holding a gun to your head?" I left the question unanswered.

MARTIN WILSON

Martin Wilson grew up in Tuscaloosa, Alabama, where both of his novels take place. He is a graduate of Vanderbilt University and the University of Florida, and his work has appeared in *Tin House, One Teen Story*, and other publications. His first YA novel, *What They Always Tell Us*, was the winner of an Alabama Author Award and a Lambda Literary Award finalist. His second novel, *We Now Return to Regular Life*, was also a finalist for the Lambda Literary Award. He currently lives in New York City, where he works as a publicist at a publishing house.

THE ONE PLACE

Martin Wilson

I write novels for teenagers. And my novels are all set in Tuscaloosa, Alabama, the only place I knew as a teenager. Over a year ago
I started writing my third novel. For a variety of reasons, I wanted to
set the story in late 1990 and early 1991. But I did have a few doubts,
and I foresaw objections from possible future editors. Why set it
then? Why not face the current reality?

As I grappled with this, I happened to go see the movie *Love,
Simon*. As a work of art, it's not breaking any ground. But in some
ways, it was revolutionary. Here was a romantic comedy about a gay
teenager—a gay version of the types of movies I loved growing up,
like *Pretty in Pink* or *Sixteen Candles*. In those movies, though, kids
like me were invisible. We didn't exist.

But we were there, all along, of course.

And that's when it dawned on me. That's when I realized
yes, I could and should set my novel in 1990. In movies and books
then, we were rarely if ever part of the story. Even in real life, our
gay teenage lives were invisible, secret, repressed. Back then, our
stories were never told. But at least one of them would be told now, I

41

decided.

Even though I have lived in New York for almost fifteen years, I still identify myself a southerner. Maybe because I want to show people that all types of people come from there—like a gay atheist liberal who isn't into football—more than any deep-seated love for the place. But maybe I hold onto my southern identity because it was the place that formed me.

There are a lot of famous quotes about "home" out there. James Baldwin wrote that "home is not a place but simply an irrevocable condition." But my favorite quote about home—or about place in general—comes from Alice Munro: "In your life there are a few places, or maybe only the one place, where something happened, and then there are all the other places." For me, that one place is Tuscaloosa. In particular, Central High School.

It's not unique for me to say I hated high school. But they were the loneliest years of my life. Those four years, I was bullied with words, though luckily not with physical acts. I had congenial relationships with many of my classmates. Teachers liked me, and I got good grades. I was on the tennis team. I had a few protective girl friends (not girlfriends) who showed me daily kindness. But on Friday nights? On weekends? I was at home, alone. Interacting with me at school was fine, for some people, I guess. But in the real world, where normal teenage things occur? I was excluded from that. The prom was something I only experienced by watching John Hughes movies. I can't even say I had an actual friend.

So, yeah, I don't look back at high school with much fondness. But I do look back with something like gratitude. Because if I hadn't been trapped in my own mind, if I hadn't lapsed into forced solitude, I'd have never put pen to paper.

Anne Tyler once said, "I write because I want more than one life." That sentence has always felt right to me. Because in writing novels about teenagers, I'm going back to that time of my life and reinserting myself—through my characters—into another life. Like I'm creating another teenage life for myself. And in my new work, set in the exact years I suffered through, I'm giving life to a story that was never told. Because even if I wasn't whooping it up at the prom, or dating a cheerleader, or doing keg stands at parties, I was there all along.

BRUCE SHENITZ

Bruce Shenitz is a writer, editor, librarian, content strategist, and taxonomist--usually not at the same time. His reporting and essays have appeared in *Out*, the *New York Times*, the *Los Angeles Times Magazine*, *Newsweek*, and several anthologies. He is the editor of the essay anthology, *The Man I Might Become: Gay Men Write About Their Fathers* that won a Lambda Literary Award. A selection of his work can be found at https://bruceshenitz.net/editing-writing/.

IN THE SHADOW OF STONEWALL

Bruce Shenitz

When I tell people that I grew up in Manhattan less than two miles from the site of the Stonewall riots they sometimes assume that my childhood was filled with unicorns and rainbows. But I was in junior high school in 1969 and like most of the rest of the world, I knew nothing of the event that became synonymous with the gay rights movement.

I think I first heard the name Stonewall a couple of years later in high school, which was actually a few blocks closer to the site. Even though my school was considered to be an activist hotbed — we marched for peace and walked out to protest against the dress code — I knew of only one student who was openly gay. He also wore a Black Panthers button. Both of those facts seemed equally exotic and dangerous to a white, Jewish adolescent from middle-class Stuyvesant Town.

When I came out in my twenties, our apartment's proximity to gay Greenwich Village may have been in the back of my family's minds. One of the first things my mother said was, "Maybe if we had moved to the suburbs this wouldn't have happened." I'm not quite sure whether she thought that greater distance from the city's premier gayborhood or merely the salubrious effects of a backyard would have straightened me out. To her credit, my mother eventually got over it. Both she and my father went to Parents and Friends of Lesbians and Gays and even became members of the gay synagogue for a couple of years in order to support it. Whatever ambivalence they may have had, they put it aside and became model parents-of-a-gay.

The original Stonewall no longer exists, but Christopher Street is still the location of many rallies, including one on June 15, 2015, the day the Supreme Court legalized same-sex marriage nationally. It also turned out to be the closest I've ever come to picking someone up at the Stonewall. When I finally got up the nerve to approach a handsome man leaning against a building just west of the now-iconic bar, he turned out to be a charming visitor from London. He also turned out to be straight. "This is not how I expected this conversation to go!" I told him, but we both had a laugh, and even had drinks while he was staying in New York.

While the Londoner and I were talking, my phone rang. It was my mother, excited about the Supreme Court decision. "Don't feel like you have to run off and rush and get married!" she mock-admonished me.

By that time my mother had been a widow for a year, and I'd lost my husband four years earlier—words I couldn't have imagined writing in 1969. In the intervening years, the Stonewall went through its own changes: it closed in 1970, and the space was occupied by businesses ranging from a pizza joint to a bagel shop, before re-opening in 1990. This current incarnation occupies only about half the space of the original and has been completely rebuilt. For many years, I thought of it as a manufactured monument, one with no genuine history other than its name and location.

But New York is often like that—the past is erased, razed, occasionally preserved, sometimes repurposed. I walk on streets I've known since childhood, but they are completely new and strange to me. And then, a sound, a smell, or a visual remnant that escaped the wrecker's ball suddenly evokes a past life.

The Stonewall and I don't really have much of a shared history, though sometimes I feel like I'm just a couple of decades away from becoming an ancient ruin, if not a National Monument. And yet, I carry histories within me as I move through the years, even as I hope to renew myself as change continues around me.

EDWARD McCANN

Edward McCann is an award-winning writer/producer and the founder and editor of Read650, a literary forum that celebrates the spoken word with live events in New York City and elsewhere. A frequent contributor to *Milieu* magazine, Ed's features and essays have been published in many literary journals, anthologies, and national magazines, including the *Sun, Country Living,* the *Irish Echo, Better Homes & Gardens, Good Housekeeping* and others. His essay, "Pregnant Again," was selected for the anthology, *Listen to Your Mother: What She Said Then, What We're Saying Now,* published by Putnam. He lives and writes in the Hudson River Valley.

TIMELINE

Edward McCann

I was born in New York City in the spring of 1963 and came of age in the mid-1970s in Florida during a sexual revolution I didn't participate in.

An altar boy raised Catholic in a large working-class family, by the time I was thirteen I was an isolated, badly dressed kid in the throes of a confusing hormonal storm, struggling to understand who and what I was—and wasn't. I knew I was different—defective, even. I didn't see myself reflected anywhere in popular culture, and I didn't identify with those men who sparked an uncomfortable glimmer of recognition. There was no Rosie or Ellen or Will & Grace. I had Charles Nelson Reilly and Paul Lynde, delivering snarky punch lines on daytime game shows.

The culture I grew up in told me that being gay was bad, depraved, and dangerous, and, as a teenager, I wasn't thinking "we" and "us;" I was thinking "them," whom I most definitely did *not* want to be.

When I was fourteen, I watched with a creeping sense of dread as wholesome, orange juice-drinking Anita Bryant, who referred to gays as "human garbage," ran the "Save Our Children" campaign to uphold discrimination based on sexual orientation. It was the same year Florida legislators approved a measure prohibiting gay adoption—and the same year I stopped going to confession and attending mass.

When I was fifteen, San Francisco Mayor George Moscone and openly gay city supervisor Harvey Milk were assassinated. At sixteen, the man who killed them was acquitted of first-degree murder—the same year a California ballot initiative sought to ban gays and lesbians from working in public schools. At seventeen, Ronald Reagan defeated Jimmy Carter by, in part, campaigning that Carter "catered" to homosexuals.

At eighteen, the news was full of frightening stories about a new "gay cancer" that the reverend Jerry Falwell, founder of the Moral Majority, said wasn't just God's punishment for homosexuals; it was God's punishment for a society that tolerated them.

By the time I was nineteen—a celibate, self-hating sophomore—it seemed my friends were all in sexual relationships, but the very idea of sex with anyone was unnerving—and potentially fatal.

After college I began my career, dated women and, at twenty-four, moved in with a woman who pursued me and claimed to appreciate my ambiguities. We shared a house, and then a bed. We shared cats and a dog and friends and many candlelit dinners, and we were very happy for a time. When I was twenty-seven, we married, and I was relieved to feel so normal, and to have achieved the life I was told I should want: I was a married man with a mortgage and a lawn to mow.

My wife and I had believed love would conquer all, but we were living a kind of lie and, after eight years together, we took it all apart. During those years, and in the years since, attitudes and the cultural landscape changed dramatically, becoming more accepting of gay women and men, electing them to office and reflecting them—us—in Hollywood films and on television shows that no longer reduced us to criminals or punchlines.

By the time I reached forty, I'd become more accepting of myself, happily settled in a loving relationship with the man I'd ultimately marry—a privilege and, perhaps more important, a constitutional right granted us by the grace of a single Supreme Court vote connected by a long, battered thread to the men and women who raised hell and energized a movement on that long-ago summer night at the Stonewall Inn.

I'm not living the life that I dreamt of, the life that I'd once wanted so badly. But these days and nights I'm living honestly as myself, no longer cloaked in shame, something I couldn't ever have imagined as a kid.

And for that, I am grateful.

ACKNOWLEDGMENTS

In addition to the contributors to this anthology, we're grateful to City Winery and its CEO Michael Dorf for hosting another Read650 live event on stage at The Loft. Thanks, too, for the production support of City Winery's Paul Bacher, Marc Coletti, and Jenny Palumbo. **CityWinery.com**

Read650's Senior Editor and Literary Ombudsman **Steven Lewis** has read virtually every submission for every live show and printed anthology for the past five years. Just counting the stories we featured, that's three hundred 650 word essays (clocking in at 1,300 pages and nearly two hundred thousand words). We can't thank you enough, Steve, and we couldn't have done all this without you. **SteveLewisWriter.com**

We are so grateful that **Jane Kaupp** of Monarch + Viceroy consulting is leading Read650's strategic marketing and communications efforts. Jane brings to us twenty years of experience marketing mass consumer brands such as Comcast, NBC News, MSNBC, CNBC, BusinessWeek, Wired, Golf Digest and Woman's Day. **MonarchAndViceroy.com**

We feel fortunate that Design Director **Diane Fokas** lends her taste and talents to shape the look and feel of Read650. Lucky for us, Diane is passionate about crafting intentional and impactful visual solutions for entrepreneurs and small businesses. **Doen.co**

Read650.org

Info @Read650.com
Facebook.com/Read650

www.ingramcontent.com/pod-product-compliance
Lightning Source LLC
Chambersburg PA
CBHW072045170626
46811CB00008B/3164